PORT OF
LONDON
SHIPPING

PORT OF LONDON SHIPPING

An Era of Change

GEOFF LUNN

TEMPUS

Frontispiece: The Port of London's most magnificent landmark: Tower Bridge has been welcoming shipping into the Upper Pool for more than a hundred years.

First published 2004

Tempus Publishing Limited
The Mill, Brimscombe Port,
Stroud, Gloucestershire, GL5 2QG
www.tempus-publishing.com

British Library Cataloguing in Publication Data.
A catalogue record for this book is available from the British Library.

ISBN 0 7524 3201 X

Typesetting and origination by Tempus Publishing Limited.
Printed in Great Britain by Midway Colour Print, Wiltshire.

Contents

Acknowledgements

I am greatly indebted to the following people and organisations for their invaluable assistance in providing me with information, advice and photographs for the collation of this book: Bob Aspinall for allowing me to research the Port of London's recent history at the Museum in Docklands' library; the Port of London Authority for providing river maps, facts and figures and inviting me to write my bi-monthly magazine feature which gave me the inspiration for this book; F.T. Everard & Sons for providing the photograph of the latest *Asperity* and the London City Mission for allowing the reproduction of the photograph of *Logos II*; Martin Klingsick, Duncan Mackenzie and Laurence Dunn, the doyen of Thames-shipping experts, for providing and agreeing to the publication of photographs of past vessels; Fotoflite for permitting me to use photographs of theirs already in my collection which have been taken from angles I could only dream of achieving; Owen Palmer and Sally Browne of the Havengore Trust for their help and advice and for providing photographs of *Havengore*, reproduced by courtesy of Museum in Docklands, PLA Collection.

Introduction

Two centuries have passed since London's first purpose-built docks were constructed. The opening of the West India Docks in 1802 marked the beginning of a period of comprehensive dock development lasting throughout much of the nineteenth century. Within a space of five years the London Docks, East India Docks and Surrey Commercial Docks opened for trading, followed later by St Katharine Dock (1828), Royal Victoria Dock (1855), Millwall Dock (1868) and the Royal Albert Dock in 1880. Tilbury Docks, on their opening in 1886, could accommodate the largest ocean ships afloat. One last piece of the dockland jigsaw was to be put in place, however, and in 1921 the King George V Dock completed the three-basin system of the Royal Docks.

By the 1930s London was the world's leading port with over 50,000 ship calls a year and a workforce of 100,000. Cargoes of every description imaginable were handled within the dock systems and by the 1,500 wharves which populated the twenty-six miles of riverside between London Bridge and Gravesend. A unique characteristic of the port was the employment of several thousand lighters to convey unloaded cargoes from visiting ships to upstream locations. The lighters would be towed in line by lighterage tugs, then manoeuvred into position by smaller launch tugs known as 'toshers'.

The Port of London was an all-motion picture of ships, tugs, lighters, cranes and dock-workers, a picture which would remain virtually unchanged until halfway into the twentieth century. Cargoes were shipped in boxes, crates, bags and barrels and handled at the quaysides via ships' hatches which were rather limited in size, a time-consuming process, meaning that ocean-going vessels would remain in port for several days.

Soon a revolution in cargo handling and ship size and design was to be forced upon shipowners due to rising operational costs and diminishing profits, and the face of the Port of London would never be the same again.

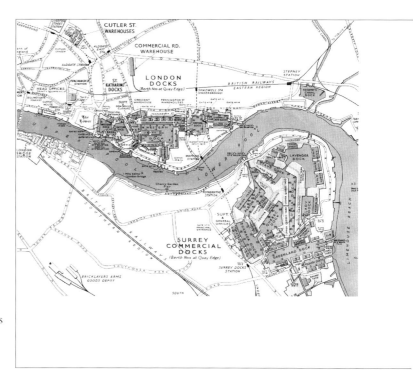

The Port of London, from London Bridge to Gallions Reach, as it was in 1962 when the docks were still in commercial use.

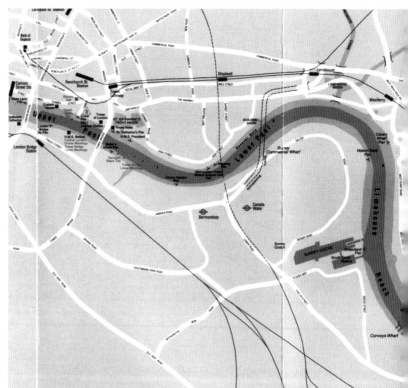

The same stretch of river in 2002; the docks have been redeveloped and new landmarks have sprung up.

8

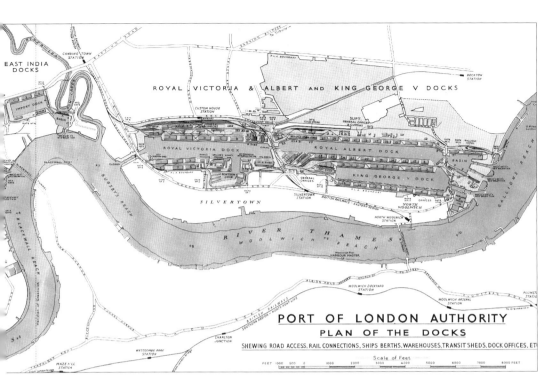

PORT OF LONDON AUTHORITY
PLAN OF THE DOCKS
SHEWING ROAD ACCESS, RAIL CONNECTIONS, SHIPS BERTHS, WAREHOUSES, TRANSIT SHEDS, DOCK OFFICES, ETC

Scale of Feet

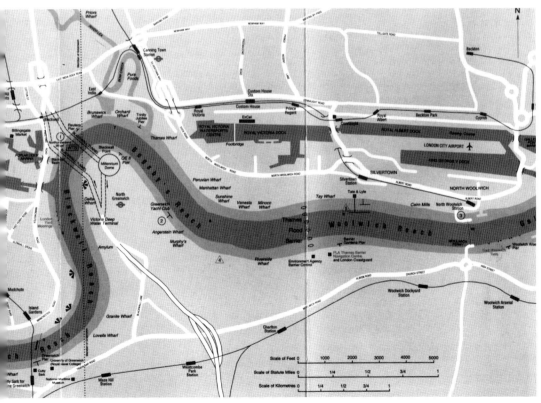

Memories of the past: A freighter discharges her cargoes at one of the many busy wharves which thronged the Thames riverside.

From the 1960s, ships were equipped with larger hatches and cargoes started to be moved in bulk. Boxes were lashed together to form unit loads discharged on pallets by forklift trucks, an idea to be extended to the evolution of the roll-on-roll-off ship. Hot on the heels of these changes the container quickly became a popular way of transporting suitable cargoes.

As ships needed to be larger, they were more expensive to run, but this could be offset by faster port turnarounds, thus allowing the ships more money-earning time at sea. The sea voyage suddenly became a link in a vast door-to-door transport chain and efficient road and rail access to and from port was absolutely vital for the chain's continuity.

The Port of London's upriver docks proved too restrictive for the new breed of large cargo ships while there was insufficient surrounding hinterland for the development of improved land access. Gradually London's docks began to close: St Katharine, London and Surrey Commercial Docks all fell quiet by 1970, and, after a ten-year reprieve, the West India and Millwall group and the mighty Royal Docks closed in 1980 and 1981 respectively. The growing success of container-handling facilities at Tilbury, the only set of docks remaining open to this day, proved to be their final downfall. In the eyes of many Londoners, this spelt the end of their port. Thousands of jobs were lost and warehouses lay empty. It seemed only a matter of time before the ships would stop sailing into the Thames.

As the twenty-first century gathers pace however, the Port of London is thriving as one of Britain's top-three ports. The overall shipping scene has shifted downstream, but well over 30,000 ship movements are recorded each year and the imaginative transformation of upriver docks and riverside wharves into commercial and residential property is encouraging two million people per annum to take to the river for business and pleasure. All these changes, though, have not been plain-sailing, especially in the eyes of experienced Thames lightermen and watermen, saddened by the disappearance of the bustling quaysides, once the foundation of their livelihoods, in favour of modern housing estates and apartment blocks.

The Port of London comprises the entire tidal Thames, ninety-five miles in all, from Teddington, west of London, to Margate on the Kent coast and Clacton-on-Sea on the coast of Essex. The stretch from Teddington down to the Nore, the outermost point of the river's estuary, comes under the auspices of the Port of London Authority. Formed in 1909, the PLA was once responsible for all London's docks, including those at Tilbury until they were subjected to a management buy-out in 1992, to be sold four years later to Forth Ports Limited for £131.6 million. The Port of Tilbury, as it is now known, is a free port, allowing its users to defer tax duties.

It was the PLA who invited me to write my first regular magazine column and more than ten years on, I still have the privilege of contributing to their news publication. My first observations of Port of London shipping can be traced back to my schoolboy days in the late 1950s however, when I would journey each week to my favourite vantage point at Gravesend. Since then I have spent many hours on or beside the river, camera in hand, enabling me to provide the majority of the photographs found in this book.

I hope that you enjoy my photographic journey through a period in time from the final years of London's upriver docks and wharves up until the present day, and even a peep into the future, a period which can surely be described as 'An Era of Change'.

Nowadays, a quiet stroll can be taken along this riverside pathway within the Pool of London, where, just a few decades ago, our daily commodities would be unloaded from ships amid the hubbub of an upriver wharf.

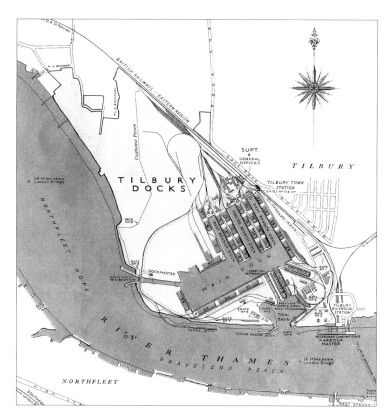

Tilbury Docks in 1962; general and refrigerated cargoes from ocean passenger and cargo liners were handled at individually numbered dockside sheds. Note the riverside Tanker Cleaning Jetty and Cargo Jetty which are now defunct.

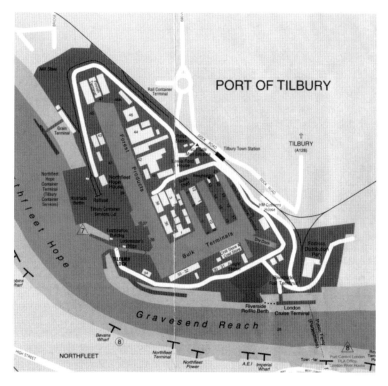

Forty years on, and now known as the Port of Tilbury, the docks and adjacent riverside feature several specially built terminals catering for the roll-on-roll-off and container trades.

one

Ocean Passenger Ships

As new methods in cargo transportation were having an important effect on the future of the Port of London's dockland, the passenger-shipping industry was experiencing its own significant changes. With emigration to Australia, New Zealand and Canada already dwindling, the introduction of long-haul jet aircraft flights led to a dramatic decline in the booking of passenger berths. Handsome ships were withdrawn from service, many consigned to the breaker's yard, and the future of ocean-liner travel looked bleak.

During the heyday of the passenger liner, elegant ships of the P&O and Orient Line fleets, which were later to merge, were frequent callers at Tilbury Landing Stage, the Port of London's principal passenger terminal. Smaller P&O passenger vessels, together with passenger/cargo ships of Royal Mail Lines, Shaw Savill, Union Castle and the New Zealand Shipping Company would berth further upstream in the Royal Docks.

By the early seventies, all these vessels had disappeared from the Port of London scene, but, happily, liner visits to the Thames continued for several more years thanks to services maintained by a number of ships of the former Soviet Union. Once the cruise-holiday phenomenon reached northern Europe and the UK, cruise ships using the Port of London's facilities also displayed the hammer and sickle, but under the operation of London-based CTC Lines who specialized in competitively priced cruises from Tilbury.

The CTC had been formed in 1966 as the Charter Travel Club, obtaining block bookings on other companies' ships for people emigrating to Australia and New Zealand, particularly those wishing to be reunited with their families. Soon CTC were chartering complete vessels, and later effectively acted as UK agents for the Black Sea Shipping Company (BLASCO), based in the Ukraine, as they concentrated on the cruise market. They changed their name to CTC Cruise Lines, but later went out of business as a result of BLASCO's financial problems.

In 1989, three-quarters of a million pounds was spent on improvements to the Tilbury Landing Stage terminal which promptly assumed the grander name of the London International Cruise Terminal. This proved a good move when major cruise lines such as Princess, Holland America and Crystal opted to take advantage of these facilities and 50,000-ton passenger ships were seen on the Thames for the first time. The cruise business in the Pool of London was healthy too, with smaller vessels berthing either downstream from Tower Bridge or tying up alongside the static naval warship HMS *Belfast* as their London base.

As the last century drew to a close, new competition from Dover and Southampton, both situated closer than London to the English Channel's shipping lanes, meant that Tilbury lost a large proportion of its passenger trade as major players in the cruise industry moved away. Nevertheless, the Pool of London has remained as busy as ever in the summer months and Tilbury receives interesting visits by small to medium-size cruise ships from a variety of nations.

The worldwide fame of London and Greenwich has made them attractive venues for ship christenings and promotional visits by newly built vessels and in this section I have featured examples of these special occasions, some of which I have had the privilege to attend.

The P&O liner *Iberia* (1954/29,614grt) sails serenely downriver from Tilbury at the start of another long voyage to Australia. Unfortunately this fine-looking ship proved mechanically unreliable over the years and was sent for breaking-up at Kaohsiung, Taiwan, when just eighteen-years old.

The classic passenger liner *Orion*, 23,696grt, steams past Thames towage tugs at Gravesend. Completed in 1935 as a two-class ship for the Orient Line, she was employed mainly in transporting emigrants to Australia in her later years, accommodating 1,697 one-class passengers. In May 1963 she became a floating hotel at Hamburg and was broken-up in Belgium later that year.

Above: Commissioned for the Soviet Merchant Fleet, the 7,494grt passenger vessel *Baltika* was christened in 1940 as *Vyacheslav Molotov.* After the war she ran between Leningrad and London under that name, being renamed *Baltika* in 1957. Soviet President Kruschev sailed in her to New York in 1960, after which there was always special interest in Suite A which he occupied. *Baltika* combined a Leningrad-Helsinki-London liner route with cruising and the occasional Government voyage to Cuba. Her accommodation was utility – a thirteen-night cruise in 1969 costing under £60! Broken-up in Pakistan in 1987.

Opposite above: The distinctive upper profile of *Orsova,* 29,794grt, highlighting the 'welsh-hat' extension to her funnel, pictured above the sheds of Tilbury Docks. Completed for the Orient Line in 1954, the liner was not easily adaptable for cruising and was broken-up at Kaohsiung in 1974.

Opposite below: Arcadia (1954/29,871grt) berthed at No.31 Shed in Tilbury Docks. As well as accommodating 679 First Class and 735 Tourist Class passengers, she could carry more than 300,000 cubic feet of general and refrigerated cargo in her six cargo holds. Like other liners on the Australia run, her open aft decks were allocated to Tourist Class passengers. Employed in cruising in her latter years, she was broken-up at Kaohsiung in 1979.

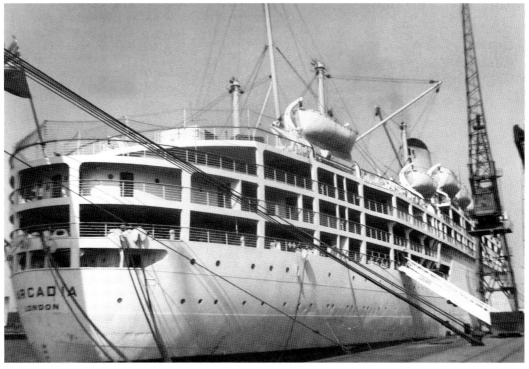

Right: As this loading broker's card shows, passenger liners would spend several days in Tilbury Docks between voyages while discharging and loading their cargoes.

Below: One for the scrapbook: the legendary Dutch liner *Rotterdam* (1959/37,783grt) berthed at Tilbury Landing Stage in 1960, her only appearance in the Thames during her distinguished career as a liner and cruise ship for the Holland America Line. She was at the time the largest post-war built liner to visit the Port of London. In 1997 she became the *Rembrandt* of Premier Cruise Lines who went bankrupt three years later. Following lay-up she is due to return to her home port of Rotterdam as a static attraction.

FEBRUARY, 1958

P&O TO AUSTRALIA VIA SUEZ

ss ARCADIA

FOR **ADELAIDE** . . . . . . due 3rd May

MELBOURNE . . . due 4th May

SYDNEY . . . . due 9th May

Refrigerated space available

LOADS	RECEIVES	CLOSES
No. 31 Shed Tilbury Dock	28th March	3rd April for all ports

Opposite above: During the days before long-haul jet travel, *Iberia* takes on passengers' baggage at Tilbury Landing Stage. On board for this voyage were members of the England cricket team, leaving for a tour of Australia.

Opposite below: Orcades (1948/28,399grt) takes on cargo in Tilbury Docks prior to embarking passengers at Tilbury Landing Stage. Her white hull, which she displays here, was changed from Orient Line's traditional corn colour following the merger of her owners with P&O during the 1960s. She was sold for breaking at Kaohsiung in 1973.

The Shaw Savill Liner *Aranda*, 18,575grt, berthed in the Royal Docks, was formerly the *Aragon* of Royal Mail Lines, from whom she was purchased in 1969. One of three identical sisters, she was completed in 1960. She was sold in May 1971 to Norwegian owners for conversion into a car carrier, renamed *Hoegh Traveller*.

The handsome buff and black funnel of *Aranda*.

It's a precarious business: crew members sunbathe high on the bows of *SS Rotterdam* during her one and only visit to Tilbury.

Accommodated within the King George V dry-dock, the P&O passenger/cargo liner *Chitral*, 13,821grt, was formerly *Jadotville* of Cie Maritime Belge. Completed in 1956, she carried up to 222 passengers between the Port of London's Royal Docks and Far Eastern ports. She was disposed of in February 1970.

A familiar visitor to the Tilbury Landing Stage for many years, the 5,035grt passenger ship *Estoniya* formed part of the nineteen-strong *Mikhail Kalinin* class constructed for the former USSR. Completed in 1960 she carried 333 First and Tourist Class passengers. She operated alongside *Baltika* on the Tilbury-Leningrad route and was employed as a cruise ship with CTC Lines. She was sold to Gals-T Joint Stock Co., Russia, in 1993 and renamed *Ekaterina II*.

Sleek black-hulled passenger ships of the Soviet Merchant Marine's *Ivan Franko* class were regular callers at Tilbury Landing Stage before the dismantling of the Soviet Union. *Alexandr Pushkin*, 19,860grt, the second of the class, was completed in 1965. Carrying 750 one-class passengers, she was employed on the Leningrad–Montreal service via London and in cruising. Transferred from the Baltic Shipping Company to the Far East Shipping Company, Vladivostok, she departed from Tilbury for the last time on 3 August 1984. She was sold to Orient Lines in 1989, refurbished and renamed *Marco Polo*. She now successfully operates as a worldwide cruise ship, including expedition-style voyages.

Opposite below: The final ship to be operated by CTC Cruise Lines, as they had then become known, *Southern Cross*, 17,270grt, (left) berthed at Tilbury with the Portuguese passenger ship *Funchal* (1961/9,563grt). *Southern Cross* was launched in 1972 as P&O's *Spirit of London*. She was transferred to Princess Cruises in 1974 and renamed *Sun Princess*. Sold to Premier Cruise Line 1988, renamed *Majestic*, then *Starship Majestic*. Bareboat chartered to CTC and renamed alongside Tilbury Landing Stage on 7 March 1995 by broadcaster Gloria Hunniford. She accommodates 750 passengers. When CTC Cruise Lines went bankrupt and ceased trading, *Southern Cross* was sold to Festival Cruises in November 1997, renamed *Flamenco*.

A ship which proved popular with her British clientele, *Kareliya* (1976/15,065grt) spent summer seasons sailing from Tilbury under the CTC banner from 1981 to 1994. Like her four sister ships, she was built at Turku, Finland, as a Soviet Union short-sea passenger vessel capable of carrying 255 cars. Allocated to the Black Sea Shipping Co. All five ships were refitted as cruise ships, the *Kareliya* on the Tyne, sailing under the name *Leonid Brezhnev* from 1982–89. Named *Kareliya* again on the advent of glasnost, she had further refits in 1989 and 1991. She accommodates 650 passengers and measures 157m x 22m. For several years she would share CTC's UK cruise programme with sister ship *Azerbaydzhan*. Following an on-board farewell party at Tilbury on 30 September 1994, she was based in Australia. Sold to K&O Shipping Ltd, Ukraine in 1997, renamed *Olvia*, under which guise she has made return visits to Tilbury.

Opposite above and below: The Ukrainian-based cruise ship *Fedor Shalyapin*, 21,406grt, made two evocative visits to Tilbury in the summer of 1994. Completed in 1955 as Cunard Line's *Ivernia* for North Atlantic service to Quebec and Montreal, she made London her home port from the late 1950s to the early 1960s (below). In 1962 she was fully reconditioned and renamed *Franconia*, thereafter employed mainly in cruising. Sold to the USSR in 1973, she was used for the Australian emigrant trade under charter to CTC, later carrying out government work and cruising. The vessel, virtually unaltered since her latter Cunard days, has been the victim of financial problems, being laid up for several years, no doubt doomed to the scrapyard.

A famous Cunard tradition retained. This sweeping staircase was still in evidence on *Fedor Shalyapin*.

The kidney-shaped swimming pool on the aft deck of *Fedor Shalyapin* had been installed in place of cargo space during the vessel's refurbishment in 1962. Despite the hot weather at the time of this picture, the pool was mysteriously empty.

Meeting bow-to-bow: *Fedor Shalyapin* and the Fred Olsen cruise ship *Black Prince*, 11,209grt (right). *Black Prince* used Tilbury's passenger facilities for a while before making Dover her UK base in 1996. Built in 1966 as a passenger/car ferry, she was converted for cruising in 1986–87. She has 450 berths and measures 143.45m x 19.60m.

Black Prince in her original guise as a 9,499grt ferry when she would lead a double life, sailing from London to the Canary Islands during the winter months while changing her name to *Venus* for her summer schedule between the Tyne and Bergen. Her identical sister *Black Watch* was similarly employed and on the Canary Islands run each ship would accommodate up to 350 passengers and bring in 3,300 tons of fruit and tomatoes for unloading at Millwall Docks.

Ready for afternoon tea: the lido café on *Black Prince* in her current role as a cruise ship.

The fifth and last of the Soviet Union's *Ivan Franko* class, *Mikhail Lermontov*, 19,872grt, made her maiden visit to the Thames in April 1972. Frequent cruises from the UK followed, together with the occasional transatlantic liner voyage, a one-way passage to Canada costing just £106. In 1982, while cruising for CTC Lines, she underwent a £10 million refit. However, on 16 February 1986, while on her first world cruise, she met an untimely end, striking underwater rocks off New Zealand and sinking without the loss of any of her passengers.

Formerly *Shota Rustaveli*, the fourth ship of the *Ivan Franko* class, *Assedo* (*Odessa* spelt in reverse) came out of lay-up at Ilychevesk, Ukraine, in 2001 to operate cruises for Russian and Ukrainian clientele, including calls at the London International Cruise Terminal. Weighing 19,567grt, she was completed in 1968. She accommodates 650 passengers, and is owned by Marchvia.

The unusual profile of *Maxim Gorkiy*, 24,981grt, was in evidence at Tilbury during the 1990s. Built as *Hamburg* for the German Atlantic Line, she entered service in March 1969. Her owners renamed her *Hanseatic* in 1973, but she was laid-up at Hamburg before being purchased by the Black Sea Shipping Company, Odessa. Initially renamed *Maksim Gorkiy*, the spelling was altered in 1992. She accommodates 650 passengers. *Maksim Gorkiy* featured in the 1974 Hollywood film *Juggernaut*, and also hosted Malta summit talks between Presidents Bush and Gorbachev in 1989. Chartered annually by German tourist operators Phoenix Reisen, she now flies the Cypriot flag.

A flying saucer or a helipad? The uniquely designed funnel of *Maxim Gorkiy* has encouraged many comparisons over the years.

A superb on-board scale model of *Maxim Gorkiy* depicts the vessel in her former Soviet Union colours.

The 9,436grt cruise ship *Daphne* was built in 1955 as the cargo liner *Port Sydney*, once a familiar sight on the Thames (see profile in the next section of this book). Sold to the J.C. Carras Group of Greece in 1972, her conversion into a passenger ship took three years. She was renamed *Akrotiri Express*, then *Daphne* on completion of the work. Taken over by Costa Cruises in 1985, and transferred to Prestige Cruises (a Costa and Sovcomflot joint venture) in 1990, she transports 422 passengers and 250 crew. She called at Tilbury three times in 1993.

In yet another guise, the *Daphne* returned to Tilbury in 1998 as the *Switzerland,* having been purchased by Swiss operator Leisure Cruises in October 1996. Her gross tonnage was amended to 15,739 and she flew the Liberian flag. In 2002 she was sold to Greek-based Majestic Cruises but this time without a name change.

Built in Finland in 1989 as a Soviet polar-research ship, *Akademik Ioffe*, 6,231grt, has sailed in another role as an expedition cruise ship under charter to Marine Expeditions Inc. of Canada, marketed as *Marine Adventurer*. She called as a cruise ship at Tilbury in the mid-1990s, carries eighty-two passengers, and has a swimming pool and saunas. There are three laboratories and underwater surveillance equipment onboard, and two large sails are stored aft of her bridge.

Akademik Ioffe in use as a cruise ship, measuring 108.4m long. Clearly in view are her rescue boat and storage for one of her sails. The crane positioned aft of her funnel is used for off-loading zodiacs and can handle cars.

The luxury cruise ship *Seabourn Pride*, 9,975grt, has been a regular summer visitor to the Pool of London since entering service in 1991. Built at Bremerhaven, she is owned by Seabourn Cruise Line, now part of the giant Carnival Group. She flies the Norwegian flag and carries up to 212 passengers. She was the first vessel to sail through Tower Bridge as it entered its second century in 1994.

The unusually designed twin funnels of *Seabourn Pride* as seen from her lido deck while the vessel is moored in the Pool of London.

The luxury cruise ship *Silver Wind*, 16,927grt, moored next to HMS *Belfast* during her first visit to the Thames in 1995. Completed in Italy towards the end of the previous year, her accommodation consists of 148 suites, eighty per cent of which have private verandas, for 296 passengers. She measures 155.81m x 21.42m. Operated by Silversea Cruises, *Silver Wind* offers cruises worldwide, featuring summer European cruises when she visits London.

Under the streamlined bows of Crystal Cruises' first ship, *Crystal Harmony*, 48,621grt. Entering service in July 1990, she carries 960 passengers in high-class accommodation, and measures 241m x 29.6m, carrying the Bahamian flag. She was a frequent visitor in the 1990s – she made eight calls in 1993. Recent schedules, though, have not included Tilbury.

The lido area of *Silver Cloud*, an identical sister to *Silver Wind*. Entering service in April 1994 she also makes the occasional summer call at Tilbury or into the Pool of London.

The suites on *Silver Cloud* are among the most well-equipped afloat.

Royal Princess, 44,348grt, makes a fine sight as she prepares to sail from Tilbury on a European cruise. Completed in 1984, she is operated by Princess Cruises, part of P&O. She accommodates 1,200 passengers in 598 cabins, and travels at 22 knots. She made several visits to the Port of London before being lured away to Dover and Southampton as her UK base ports.

A close-up study of *Royal Princess* berthed at the London International Cruise Terminal. The Gravesend-Tilbury ferry would often take slight detours during its crossings to enable its passengers to appreciate the size of modern-day cruise ships.

At approximately 41,000 gross tons, the Norwegian Cruise Line's *Dreamward* was the largest passenger vessel to pass through the Thames Barrier when she arrived direct from her builders for a promotional visit to Greenwich on 6 November 1992. She measured 190.05m in length and had accommodation for 1,246 passengers, but, with her sister *Windward*, she was lengthened to 229.85m in 1998, enabling her to carry 1,748 passengers. Renamed *Norwegian Dream* on re-entering service, she now weighs in at 50,764grt.

The all-teak terraced upper-lido deck of *Dreamward*.

THE DREAMWARD

Luncheon
Friday, 6th November 1992
Greenwich, London

Menu

SEAFOOD COCKTAIL, SAUCE LOUISE

———

CLEAR OXTAIL SOUP DOUBLE WITH CHEESE STRAW

———

M/S DREAMWARD SALAD

HEART OF BUTTER LETTUCE, YELLOW PEAR TOMATO

ALFALFA SPROUTS, SLICED RADISHES AND WATERCRESS LEAVES

BALSAMICO DRESSING

———

SORBET POIRE WILLIAMS

———

BROILED FILLET OF FRESH SALMON

LEMON BUTTERSAUCE GARNISHED WITH TOMATO CONCASSE

PARSLEY POTATOES, BROCCOLI SPEARS

OR

MEDALLIONS OF VEAL "FOUR SEASONS"

NATURAL JUICE

BUTTERED NOODLES

———

TIRAMISU

ITALIAN STYLE CHEESECAKE

———

COFFEE

A mouth–watering selection to commemorate a special day.

The Holland America cruise ship *Statendam* (1993/55,451grt), the fifth passenger ship to bear the name, first arrived in the Port of London in June 1993 at the end of a thirty-five-day Grand Europe cruise, fares costing from US$7,250. Built by Fincantieri in Italy, she measures 219.3m x 30.8m, and carries a maximum of 1,629 passengers in 633 cabins. She made several further calls during the 1990s.

The fourth *Statendam*, 24,294grt, entered service in 1957 and made only one call at Tilbury, on 8 August 1961, during a seven-day cruise from Copenhagen. Fares ranged from just £23 10s to £80! She was sold by Holland America Line to Paquet Cruises in 1980 and renamed *Rhapsody*. Purchased by Regency Cruises in 1986, she was renamed *Regent Star*, but when her owners became bankrupt in 1995 she was laid-up at Eleusis Bay, Greece as *Sea Harmony* awaiting her fate.

There is no mistaking the name of her owners, clearly displayed beneath the futuristically designed funnel of *Statendam (V)*.

The fifth *Statendam's* magnificent lido area with its retractable roof in closed position.

Top-rated cruise ship *Royal Viking Sun*, 37,845grt at Tilbury International Cruise Terminal in 1997. Delivered for the now-disbanded Royal Viking Line in November 1988, she called at Greenwich on her maiden voyage. She carries 768 passengers, has a top speed of 21 knots, and is 225.55m long. She was transferred to Cunard Line in 1994, then to Seabourn Cruise Line as *Seabourn Sun* in 1999. She was eventually transferred again in 2002 to Holland America Line and renamed *Prinsendam*.

The lido area of *Royal Viking Sun*, showing her main swimming pool with swim-up bar.

A frequent visitor to the Thames since her completion in 1998, the German cruise ship
Deutschland carries up to 650 passengers in stylish accommodation. At 22,500grt she is the fifth and
largest vessel to bear the name, although with a length of 175.3m, she is shorter than the third
Deutschland built in 1900. She is owned by Peter Deilmann Reederei.

Japan's largest cruise ship called into the Port of London for the first time in the spring of 2000.
The 28,717grt *Asuka*, owned by the NYK Group, berthed at Greenwich as part of a world cruise.
She measures 190m x 24.7m, and carries 584 passengers in 292 cabins. Delivered by Mitsubishi
Heavy Industries in 1991, she has a top speed of 21 knots.

The twin-hulled cruise ship *Radisson Diamond* (1992/20,295grt) called briefly at the Tilbury Landing Stage prior to her naming ceremony at Greenwich. Owned by Diamond Cruise Inc. and marketed by Radisson Hotels International, her design is officially described as SWATH – Small Waterplane Area Twin Hull. At 128m long and with an overall width of 31.4m, she carries 354 passengers and 192 crew.

With a little help from her friends, opera singer Dame Kiri Te Kanawa prepares to break a bottle of champagne on one of *Radisson Diamond's* hulls when naming the cruise ship at Greenwich on 28 May 1992. The event differed from the normal ceremony, as both of the ship's hulls were christened individually.

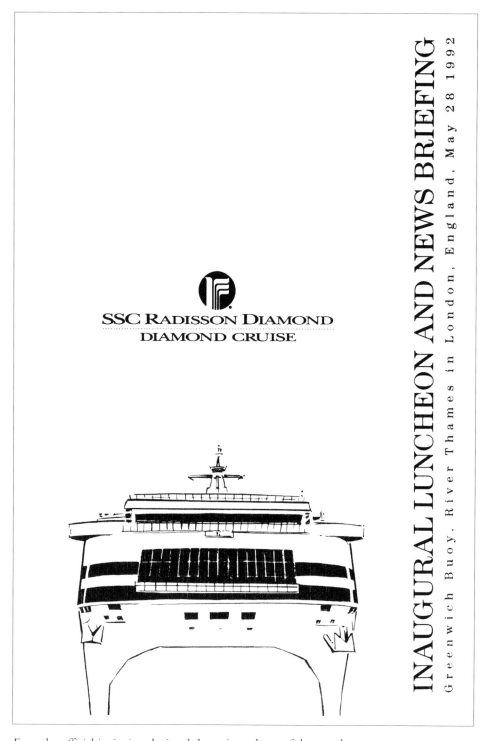

Even the official invitation depicted the unique shape of the vessel.

Looking between the hulls: *Radisson Diamond's* propulsion is housed in both hulls, while her deep draught (7.92m) and narrowness of the hulls at waterline level notably improve her stability.

Swan Hellenic's *Minerva* moored alongside HMS *Belfast* in the Pool of London. Constructed on a Russian-built hull in a Genoa shipyard, the 12,500grt ship was designed to carry about 300 passengers and first arrived in the Thames in the summer of 1996 to be named by HRH The Duchess of Gloucester in the West India Dock. Purchased by Saga in 2003 and renamed *Saga Pearl*, she measures 133m long and travels at 17.5 knots.

The 51,044grt cruise ship *Crystal Symphony* was delivered to Crystal Cruises in early 1995, calling at Tilbury on 23 April that year after a ninety-six-day world cruise. Offering five-star accommodation for 975 passengers served by 545 crew members, she is 238m long and 30.2m wide. Her public rooms include Oriental and Italian restaurants and a Palm Court lounge. Visited the Thames in 1999 but since transferred to Dover and Southampton.

Smaller cruise ships, such as *Seabourn Pride*, capable of navigating the Thames as far as the Upper Pool, normally tie-up alongside HMS *Belfast*.

On a blustery morning in April 2002 the first-ever residential ship *The World*, 43,525grt, arrived at Tilbury International Cruise Terminal direct from her trials. She later moored upstream at Greenwich for three days, enabling prospective residents and other guests to inspect her. She has 110 apartments, allowing an average occupancy of 390 residents, and eighty-eight guest suites. She measures 196.35m x 29.80m. She operates a continuous worldwide itinerary, many of her port calls coinciding with major international events.

Residents at sea meet residents ashore: the most expensive apartment block afloat moored in the Thames near residential Greenwich. A riverbus is ready to ferry residents and guests upstream to Tower Pier. Note the slab-sided superstructure and hull of *The World*, a common design feature of the modern ocean passenger ship.

Left: Contrasting the old and the new: *The World's* own helipad, positioned at her bow, with the former tea clipper *Cutty Sark*, Greenwich's famous tourist attraction, in the background.

Below: Living in luxury: the dining section of a residential apartment on *The World*.

The ultimate address: *The World's* name displayed above her residents' private balconies.

One of the most luxurious modern-day cruise ships, *Silver Whisper*, 28,258grt, made local news when she visited the Port of London in July 2001 during her maiden voyage. Operated by Silverseas Cruises, her accommodation is brimming with understated elegance, every cabin having a marble bathroom. She carries 382 passengers and 295 crew, and has 194 cabins, 168 with private balconies. She measures 185m x 24.9m.

The unimaginatively named 30,277grt cruise ship *R 7* made just one visit to the Port of London –
to be laid-up in Tilbury Docks. When her owners Renaissance Cruises went bankrupt this
181m-long vessel and her seven identical sisters had to find buyers. *R 7* stayed at Tilbury from
October to December 2001 when she was acquired by a company calling itself Cruise Invest
Seven. She has since been chartered to German operators Delphin Seereisen and renamed *Delphin
Renaissance*. Completed in September 2000, she carries 684 passengers at a top speed of 18 knots.

Snap! Well, almost. *R 8*, sister of the *R 7*, was purchased by P&O for their upmarket cruise
subsidiary Swan Hellenic and renamed *Minerva II*. On her first visit to London in the summer of
2003 she became the largest passenger ship ever to moor in the Lower Pool. She replaced the
smaller *Minerva*, then Swan Hellenic's only other vessel in service, increasing the company's
available berth capacity by 300. Completed in 2001, her gross tonnage increased to 30,777
following a refit.

two

Ocean
Freighters

Radical changes in cargo-handling methods have resulted in the steady disappearance of the conventional cargo ship over the years and the emergence of container ships, roll-on-roll–off (ro-ro) ships and vehicle carriers as regular visitors to the Port of London. The average-sized conventional cargo ship was around 8,000 gross tons in the days of London's docks with the occasional larger ship of 10-13,000 tons. Products such as meat, fruit and vegetables were brought in from Australia, New Zealand, South Africa and South America and some vessels had refrigerated holds within their cargo space. A few larger ships were adapted to carry containers in addition to conventional 'break-bulk' cargo, but these were gradually sold on or scrapped as larger, faster and more cost-effective vessels came on to the scene.

It was on 2 June 1968 that a particular ship's arrival influenced the future of ship-handling methods within the Port of London. Berthing in Tilbury Docks, the United States Lines' container ship *American Lancer*, the first of a new class of vessel, was greeted by just fifteen dock workers who proceeded to unload her in thirteen hours. Had the new ship been carrying break-bulk cargo rather than containers, it was estimated that 176 dockers would have been required to do the same job.

Today, ships of over 20,000 tons are commonplace in the Thames, while some container ships and car carriers exceed 50,000 tons. There may be far fewer commercial ships visiting the port, but this is offset by the sheer capacity of the modern-day vessel, requiring, in turn, more expansive berthing facilities. Consequently the port's main commercial activities now centre around Tilbury, where new purpose-built terminals have been constructed. The combination of these new facilities and the sophistication of on-board cargo-handling equipment ensures ship turnarounds of just a few hours.

The Port of London's first dedicated container terminal was completed in 1969. Initially operated by Overseas Containers Ltd (OCL), it is now managed and operated by Tilbury Container Services. It consists of the original No.39 Berth and No.41 Berth in Tilbury's inner docks, and following an extension in 2002, a 600m riverside berth in Northfleet Hope, allowing two large container ships to be handled simultaneously, including vessels capable of carrying more than 4,000 standard-sized twenty-foot equivalent units (TEU). Immediately upstream is Tilbury Grain Terminal which also dates back to 1969 and frequently welcomes large bulk carriers.

Within the Port of Tilbury's docks, recent years have seen the opening of two terminals specialising in forest and paper products: the Finnish Terminal at 45/47 Berths and the Interforest Terminal at 44 Berth. Just outside the docks, immediately upstream from the Tilbury Landing Stage, Hyundai Merchant Marine have opened car-import facilities with a 220m berth.

Upriver at Plaistow, the jetty at Tate & Lyle's Silvertown sugar terminal has been extended over the years so that bulk raw sugar can be discharged from ocean freighters directly into their works. Up until the 1960s, sugar used to be unloaded downriver at Dagenham Dock and jetties at Purfleet and Erith and transhipped up to Plaistow by barge.

The days when ocean freighter fleets were owned and operated by single companies have long gone. Container ships in particular tend to be operated by large consortia nowadays, often subject to transfer or charter between companies operating similar routes and services. Consequently, some vessels visiting the Port of London acquire a whole string of name changes during their careers.

Two typically busy views of the Royal Docks during the 1960s. Above: the newly completed German fruit ship *Persimmon* (1967/6,501grt), operated by F. Laeisz, with rows of lighters in the foreground. She became the Panamanian-registered *Grand United* in 1979 and was broken up at Lisbon in 1985. Below: The Dutch general-cargo liner *Katendrecht* (1961/8,845grt), owned by Phs Van Ommeren. She was sold in 1975, renamed *Cabo Santa Anna*, then *Cabo Santa* in 1989. In the background another freighter is berthed on the opposite quay.

The Greek-registered freighter *Eurybates* (1961/9,659grt) receives assistance from the Thames tug *Crested Cock* (1935/177grt) as she arrives in the Port of London. Owned by Cia San Basilio SA of Piraeus, she measures 164m x 19.2m and has steam turbines giving her a top speed of 17 knots. She was sold to owners in Kuwait 1977 and renamed *Al Wasseem*. She arrived at Karachi for breaking-up in November 1979.

The cargo liner *Hardwicke Grange* (1961/10,338grt) was involved in the frozen-meat trade, sailing from the Royal Docks on the London to South America service maintained by ships of Houlder Bros Co. Ltd. Like many conventional cargo vessels constructed within a decade of the container ship boom, she did not enjoy a long life. She was sold and renamed *Jacques*, and broken-up at Kaohsiung in 1979.

FEBRUARY, 1958

P&O TO AUSTRALIA VIA SUEZ

SS NUDDEA

MELBOURNE	due 8th April
GEELONG	due 13th April
SYDNEY	due 18th April
PORT KEMBLA	due 23th April

Refrigerated space available

LOADS	RECEIVES	CLOSES
16/18 Shed Royal Albert Dock	28th February	8th March for Sydney & Port Kembla 10th March for other ports

A loading broker's card from the dockland era. Nowadays far larger ships than the 8,596grt *Nuddea* can be turned round in a matter of hours.

Spanish ships of the Aznar Line maintained a regular service between the Canary Islands and New Fresh Wharf, situated on the north bank of the Thames immediately downstream from London Bridge. Known as the *Monte* ships as their names were prefixed *Monte*, they brought in canned goods and fresh fruit. During one departure from London the 8,392grt *Monte Urquiola* managed to get herself pinned sideways under London Bridge for several hours before commencing her voyage. She was sold to Singapore owners in 1975, and became the *Climax Garnet*. She arrived in Pakistan for breaking in December 1977.

Soon after the Second World War, Blue Star Line took delivery of four cargo/passenger liners from Cammell Laird's Birkenhead shipyard for their South American service. Each ship had accommodation for up to sixty-nine First Class passengers. *Argentina Star*, 10,716grt, pictured above, taking on cargo in the Royal Docks for another voyage to Buenos Aires, was completed in 1947. Another member of the quartet, *Paraguay Star*, 10,722grt, (below) made her maiden voyage in 1948 and saw service until 1969 when she was scrapped at Hamburg.

Above: On-board *Argentina Star* during her latter days. She arrived at Kaohsiung in October 1972 for breaking-up.

Below: Featured in Chapter One in her present shape as a cruise ship, *Port Sydney* (1955/9,189grt) maintained a regular cargo service between the Royal Docks and Australian ports. She measures 162.45m x 21.34m with a top speed of 17 knots and has refrigerated cargo holds and diesel engines. She was sold for conversion into a cruise ship in 1972.

Houlder Bros' cargo ship *Hardwick Grange* from another angle: on her builders' trials following her completion at the Hebburn yard of Hawthorn Leslie. She measured 149m x 20.1m. Powered by steam turbines, she had a service speed of 16 knots.

Opposite above: In 1950 a new British shipping company, the Sugar Line Ltd, was formed by Tate & Lyle and the United Molasses Co. in response to the beginning of bulk transportation of raw sugar. *Sugar Refiner*, 5,104grt, completed in December 1958, would frequently call at Tate & Lyle's Silvertown refinery. She was sold to Finnish owners in 1967 and renamed *Arcadia*. In 1972 she became the Cypriot-owned *Irenes Faith*, in 1974 the *Elarkadia* (Greek-owned), in 1978 the *Navisailor*, then *Sailer II* (both Cypriot-owned) and finally in 1979 she was renamed *Molly* (Panamanian flag). She was broken-up at Split in 1986.

Opposite below: Through the green leaves of summer the Nigerian cargo liner *River Mada* (1979/10,984grt) is pictured at her lay-up berth at Tilbury Docks prior to disposal by her owners. Vessels of the Nigerian National Line left the Port of London scene by the late 1980s.

Between 1969 and 1971 a new class of container ship, the *Lancer*-class, owned by United States Lines, maintained a weekly service into the Port of London from the North American ports of New York, Norfolk and Baltimore, unloading at No.40 Berth, Tilbury Docks. One of the last of the class to be built, *American Astronaut* (1969/18,876grt) is pictured arriving off Tilbury on her maiden voyage. Sold to Puerto Rican owners in 1989, she was renamed *Guayama*.

The distinctive superstructure of *American Liberty* (1968/18,876grt), an early *Lancer*-class vessel and one of the world's first purpose-built fully cellular container ships. She measures 214m x 27.43m, has a top speed of 23 knots and carries 1,210 TEU. She has eight holds forward of superstructure and three aft. She was renamed *Sea-Land Liberty* in 1987, *Sea-Land Discovery* in 1988 and *CSX Discovery* in 2000.

Swedish-flagged ships of the Johnson Line berthed at No.4 Berth Tilbury Docks during the 1970s. Built at Turku in Finland, *Annie Johnson*, 16,288grt, was a part-container/part-general-cargo vessel sailing to the Pacific coast of North America and carried up to 750 TEU. She was sold in 1986 and renamed *Regent Moon*, and sold again in 1988 when she was renamed *Alexandra*. In 1990 she was acquired by the Italian cruise company Costa Cruises and converted into a cruise ship. She re-entered service in January 1993 as *Costa Allegra*.

With emissions from her powerful steam turbines billowing behind her, Overseas Container Line's first vessel, the 26,767grt *Encounter Bay*, leaves Tilbury for another long voyage 'down-under'. On completion in Hamburg in 1969 she was the world's largest container ship. Within a year she was joined by five sisters. She measures 227.38m x 30.48m and has a top speed of 21.5 knots.

A member of the second generation of container ships built for Associated Container Transportation Ltd (ACT), the 24,212grt *ACT 5* was delivered by German shipbuilders Bremer Vulkan in 1972. In addition to carrying up to 1,294 TEU, including refrigerated boxes, she had a general-cargo hold positioned forward served by a forty-ton crane. Her registered owners were Blue Star Line, and in 1991 she was renamed *Sydney Star* and changed to Blue Star colours. With her three sisters, the former *ACTs 3, 4* and *6*, she was sent for scrapping at Shanghai in 2003, spelling the end for the Blue Star Line.

Opposite below: The container ship *Heemskerk* (1978/51,982grt) flies the Dutch flag and has passed twenty-five years in service. Named *Transvaal* until 1987, she is owned by P&O Nedlloyd BV, Rotterdam, and carries a maximum of 3,126 TEU. With seven cellular holds, she measures 258.53m x 32.31m and has a top speed of 23 knots.

Much larger container ships were soon in service, operated by various company consortia. *Pegasus Bay*, 52,055grt, started life as *City of Durban* in 1978 under the ownership of Ellerman Lines. In 1983–84 she sailed under the name *Portland Bay* and from 1985 to 1990 as the *ACT 8*. She measured 258m x 32.31m and had a top speed of 21 knots. She carried 2,870 TEU. *Pegasus Bay's* ownership transferred to P&O Containers, then P&O Nedlloyd following the merger between P&O and Royal Nedlloyd NV in 1995. She was one of several ships to be replaced by a new *Albatross* class of high-capacity vessels.

For the majority of her career the 43,704grt container ship *New Zealand Pacific* bore the accolade of being New Zealand's largest ship. Built in 1978 for the New Zealand Shipping Corporation, she was flagged out briefly as the *Tui* in 1989, but otherwise flew the flag of her home country until 1996 when she was absorbed into the giant P&O Nedlloyd fleet. She measured 248.60m x 32.31m and had twelve cellular holds with a capacity of 2,344 TEU, including 1,071 refrigerated. She was demolished in the Far East in 2003.

The Greek-registered *Avlis*, 10,287grt, discharges bulk raw sugar at the jetty of Tate & Lyle's Silvertown terminal. Built in Japan 1979 and owned by Mediterranean Galaxy SA, she measures 145.52m x 21.04m, with a top speed of 14.5 knots.

Surely one of the most unusual deep-sea vessels to visit the Port of London, *Baco-Liner 2*, (1980/22,345grt) sails from Tilbury and the near-Continent to West African ports. Her Baco-Liner (BArge-COntainer-Carrier) concept enables her not only to carry 652 TEU but to act as the mother ship for three sets of four 24m barges, one set positioned in her loading port, one on-board and one in her discharging port. She measures 205m x 28.5m with a top speed of 15 knots. She is owned by Seereederei Baco-Liner GmbH. Two similar ships, *Baco-Liner 1* and *Baco-Liner 3*, operate alongside her.

One of four sisters, known as the 'Big Whites', *S A Helderberg*, 52,615grt, links Tilbury's container terminal and continental ports with South Africa. This service was transferred from Southampton. Completed in 1978, she has a maximum capacity of 2,464 TEU and measures 258.5m x 32.3m, with a top speed of 19 knots. She has accommodation for ten passengers.

The remarkable high-tech specifications of the 20,154grt *Ostrand* demonstrate how far methods of transporting forest products have advanced in recent years. Completed in a Seville shipyard in 1996 she maintains a twice-weekly service between Scandinavian ports and No.44 Berth Tilbury Docks with two sister vessels, *Obbola* and *Ortviken*. There are no cranes, not even trailers, but cargo is lashed on to wheel-less cassettes loaded via the ship's stern. She has a total capacity of 140 cassettes, and measures 156m x 23.5m. She can operate with a crew of ten.

At her berth in Tilbury Docks the Grimaldi ro-ro ship *Repubblica di Genova* (1988/42,567grt) loads via her large stern ramp/door for South American ports. She can carry up to 1,350 TEU and 3,500 cars and has comfortable accommodation for fifty passengers. Lengthened in 1990 to 216.08m x 30.40m, she has a top speed of 18.5 knots, and carries the Italian flag.

One of the largest vessels to sail regularly into the Port of London, *Grande America*, 56,642grt, was delivered to the Grimaldi group in December 1998. She measures 214m x 32.25m. A versatile ship, she carries cars, vans and larger vehicles, forest products, containers and general cargo. In total she can transport up to 1,321 TEU and 3,515 cars. She accommodates twelve passengers, and is the first of a class of technically advanced ro-ro ships sailing from UK and Continental ports to Brazil and Argentina.

On her completion at Swan Hunter's Newcastle-upon-Tyne yard in 1973, P&O's 41,814grt *Remuera* was the world's largest and fastest refrigerated-container ship. Initially chartered to ACT (Australia) and Australian National Line, she transferred to OCL in 1977 and was renamed *Remuera Bay*. She measures 252.03m x 32.14m and carries 2,074 TEU (including 1,201 refrigerated) at a top speed of 21 knots. She was renamed *Berlin Express* in 1993, and *Press* in 2002. Two earlier deep-sea ships named *Remuera* were owned by the New Zealand Shipping Company.

Continuing the *Remuera* tradition, *P&O Nedlloyd Remuera*, 45,803grt, the first of a new *Albatross* class of seven vessels, became the largest refrigerated-container ship afloat on leaving her Korean builders' yard in 2001. Employed on P&O Nedlloyd's Europe–New Zealand service, she can carry 4,112 TEU, 1,300 refrigerated. She is 281m long, with a service speed of 23.5 knots. Designed, with other ships of the class, to replace earlier-generation container ships.

Another bulk carrier employed in the importing of raw sugar cane to the Silvertown terminal, the 14,922grt *Maritime Trader* was built in Japan in 1985. Until 2001 she was named *Arctic Trader*. She measures 159.76m x 25.23m with a draught of 10.24m. Owned by Hong Kong Trader Nav. Co. Ltd, she has four holds and a top speed of 13.5 knots.

A comfortable lounge is a feature of the facilities provided for passengers travelling on the Grimaldi group's large ro-ro ships.

A new ro-ro service linking Tilbury Docks with Jeddah and Far East ports was introduced in 1996 by Hyundai Merchant Marine (Europe) Ltd utilising Pure Car and Truck Carriers (PCTC). A spacious berth at Tilbury Riverside, just upstream from the Tilbury Landing Stage, was later opened by the company where *Hyundai No 205*, 42,427grt, is unloading Hyundai vehicles. Built in 1987, she sailed under the name *Eurasian Beauty* 1990–93. She measures 183.90m x 30.64m and has a top speed of 19.8 knots.

A multi-purpose ro-ro vessel, *Roxanne*, 32,173grt, was built in 1976 in Helsinki as the *Komsomolsk* for Russian owners. In 1995 she was renamed *Kotlini* under Cypriot registry and in 1997 she was renamed *Nicole*, with the flag of St Vincent. Acquired by present owners, Rosewater Maritime Inc. (Managers – Egon Oldendorff OG) in 2000, she measures 205.80m x 31.15m. She has a quarter-stern door/ramp and four decks. She carries up to 242 cars and eighty-one trailers and 1,346 TEU. She supplemented Grimaldi ships on South American service.

With business at the Hyundai ro-ro terminal expanding rapidly in the new millennium, a service for the importation of vehicles from Turkey was launched by United European Car Carriers (UECC) using chartered tonnage. *Asian Breeze* (1983/28,117grt) is one of several Wallenius-owned vessels employed. She carries up to 3,070 cars on ten decks. She measures 164m x 28.05m, and has a top speed of 18 knots.

Operated by Safmarine on the Europe Pakistan India Consortium (EPIC) service linking the Indian sub-continent with northern Europe, *Safmarine Kimley* (1996/37,549grt) is owned by a Bremen-based company and flies the German flag. Built by Daewoo Heavy Industries as *Sea-Land Mistral*, she measures 241m x 32.2m and carries 3,660 TEU at a top speed of 24 knots.

Representing the ultimate in modern adaptability, *Pauline Russ* (1999/10,488grt) is capable of transporting trailers and loaded cassettes as well as paper products, general cargo and containers. Apart from the containers, which are loaded by the ship's crane, cargoes are handled through the ship's stern doors. One of three *Sietas*-class vessels built for Transfennica, a Finnish company owned by the country's three main paper exporters, she has a minimum service speed of 21 knots, contributing to a three-calls-a-week service from Nos 45/47 Berths in the Port of Tilbury to Finnish ports.

Passing giants: *SA Winterberg* (1978/52,615grt), another of Safmarine's 'Big Whites' sailing for South Africa (left) and the inward-bound *P&O Nedlloyd Remuera* (2001/45,803grt) on one of her first voyages from New Zealand, dwarf an Adsteam towage tug.

three

Ocean Tankers and
Miscellaneous Ships

Before the recent closure of Shellhaven, three oil refineries were in operation within the Port of London's boundaries. Situated on the northerly banks of the Thames in Essex, the remaining two refineries, Coryton and Thameshaven, are capable of receiving Very Large Crude Carriers (VLCCs) at their deep-water berths.

Further upriver, Tilbury Tanker Repair Jetty, situated close to where the Tilbury riverside ro-ro terminal now operates, would receive visits from ocean-going tankers for tank cleaning, becoming, during the sixties and seventies, the largest vessels to pass Gravesend.

Over the years the Port of London has frequently hosted promotional and courtesy calls from various types of ocean ships, ranging from warships to cable ships and even hospital ships, creating much interest during their time in port.

Mobil Tankers' 1969-built *Mobil Pegasus*, 112,657grt, berthed at Coryton, a 370-acre site opened in 1953. The vessel, which measured one-fifth of a mile in length, caused considerable interest during the 1970s when she was navigated up the Thames to Tilbury Tanker Repair Jetty, requiring her to turn around in the river at Northfleet Hope, thus becoming the largest vessel to sail upriver beyond Gravesend.

The establishment of a methane gas terminal at Canvey Island proved a successful venture for a number of years. Two ships, *Methane Princess* and *Methane Progress* (the latter seen here berthing at Canvey), were purpose-built for bringing the methane gas in from north Africa in a liquid state, made possible by its carriage at extremely low temperatures. The gas, having reverted to its natural state at Canvey, would then be piped through Britain's domestic gas-grid system. *Methane Progress* (1964/21,876grt), owned by the British Gas Board, was laid up at Falmouth in July 1981 on the conclusion of the venture and was towed to Spanish ship-breakers in August 1986.

The 4,804grt missionary ship *Logos II* made two lengthy visits to the Port of London during the 1990s. Owned by Educational Book Exhibits Ltd, she has voyaged worldwide, carrying up to 139 international personnel. On-board is a vast book exhibition hall containing 4,000 volumes. Built in 1968 as the Spanish ferry *Antonio Lazaro*, she was purchased for her new duties in 1988.

An unusual twenty-first century visitor: The Japanese 'Large Patrol' vessel *Kojima* sails down the Thames following a courtesy visit. Commissioned in March 1993 for the Maritime Safety Agency, she is employed as a training ship. She has 2,650 tons displacement, a complement of 118 and a range of 7,000 miles at 15 knots.

The Port of London has played host to a countless number of warships, from home and abroad, making courtesy visits to England's capital city. In recent years the majority have tied up alongside HMS *Belfast* but the Royal Navy aircraft carrier *Invincible* was too large to berth further upstream than at Greenwich. The 210m-long ship, which created considerable interest as she sailed past Gravesend, dates back to July 1979.

The British cable ship *Mercury*, owned by Cable & Wireless Ltd, at Greenwich during the 1960s after loading 1,260 nautical miles of telephone cable prior to sailing to the Far East for the completion of the Hong Kong/Guam section of the South East Asia Commonwealth telephone cable. Built by Cammell Laird, Birkenhead, the 9,048grt vessel entered service in 1962, visiting the Thames to load cable for her maiden voyage. She was broken up by Spanish ship-breakers, arriving in tow from Bristol in December 1997.

The world's largest privately owned non-governmental hospital ship, *Anastasis*, 11,695grt, has made several appearances in the Port of London, including a special visit to London's Docklands in September 1998 in celebration of the twentieth anniversary of Mercy Ships, her owners. Equipped with operating theatres, a dental clinic and x-ray unit, she even has a school for the children of her crew members. Formerly the 1953-built Italian liner *Victoria*, she was purchased in 1978. She measures 148.9m x 20.7m, with 425 berths and three cargo holds.

A rare view of HMS *Belfast* away from her Pool of London mooring. In June 1999 the preserved Second World War cruiser was towed stern-first downriver on her way to Portsmouth for an inspection and recoating of her hull, taking a brief pause at Tilbury Landing Stage.

Built in Finland for the Cable & Wireless Marine Company, the 14,227grt *Cable Innovator* has made courtesy visits to Tilbury, Greenwich and the Pool of London since entering service in 1995 as the world's largest cable vessel. Cable-laying work is carried out over her stern for which she can carry up to 10,000km of cable. Eighty single cabins are provided for officers, ratings and customer representatives.

Cable Innovator at Tilbury Landing Stage in 1995 after sailing in direct from her builders. Two lines of cable are laid through her stern sheaves while the large 'A'-frame controls the launching and recovery of the cable.

Dressed overall for Tower Bridge's 100th birthday party, the Royal Yacht *Britannia* moored in the Upper Pool in 1994. Three years later she visited London for the last time, departing on 21 November 1997 for decommissioning at Portsmouth. She is now a popular tourist attraction at Leith, Edinburgh.

four

Short-sea Ships

Before their demise, the uppermost of London's docks and riverside wharves were home to small cargo vessels which sailed in from the near-Continental ports, the Iberian Peninsular, Baltic countries and Ireland. Butter and bacon came from Denmark, wines from France and Spain, and Guinness from across the Irish Sea. Downstream at Tilbury, Swedish Lloyd maintained a regular passenger/cargo service to and from Gothenburg. It is believed that passenger ships used to run on this route even before the start of the twentieth century. In contrast, the final ship employed on the service was equipped to carry containers.

It was the beginning of the container era which led to a dramatic change in the design of the short-sea ship. Suddenly a freight terminal at Dartford found itself as the Port of London's busiest short-sea berth, handling containers and unaccompanied trailers. Roll-on-roll-off ships replaced the old cargo ships and these, in turn, have notably increased in size over the past three decades, with a class of vessels exceeding 20,000 gross tons now in service.

The expansion of the Dartford terminal, now known as Thames Europort, and the phenomenal growth of purpose-built ro-ro facilities at nearby Purfleet for the Belgian ro-ro specialist Cobelfret have resulted in regular services to and from the near-Continent involving the carriage of containers, trailers and cars. The import and export of new cars has become a major part of the short-sea trade, Ford's works at Dagenham featuring as a scheduled stop on some services.

At Tilbury Docks and the Northfleet Hope container terminal, small 'feeder' container vessels take on containers which have been shipped in by large ocean-going container ships for onward shipment to smaller British and continental ports, another example of the transformation of short-sea shipping.

A twenty-first century scene in Gravesend Reach: Dart Line's outward-bound short-sea ro-ro vessel *Dart 4* (1984/9,088grt) passing the multi-purpose deep-sea ship *Pauline Russ* en route from Finland. Stern-loading roll-on-roll-off ships are now the mainstay of much of the Port of London's sea trade.

Ships on the long-established London-Gothenburg passenger-cargo route of Swedish Lloyd
(Svenska Lloyd Rederi A/B) used a specially constructed terminal at No.26 Berth Tilbury Docks
from the 1960s, one of the ships using the berth being *Saga* (1966/7,889grt). She carried
408 passengers, 100 cars and 100 containers, and measured 141m x 21m. She was twin-screw with
a top speed of 18 knots. She was joined by sister vessel *Svea* which closed the service in 1978,
having replaced *Saga*, taking her name, in 1972.

British-flagged ships of the United Baltic Corporation were regular callers at Hays Wharf, on the
south bank of the Thames close to London Bridge, and at Surrey Commercial Docks. One of
their grey-hulled cargo vessels was *Baltic Vanguard* (1966/1,785grt), their first side-loading ship and
their first to have steel hatch covers. She measures 93.9m x 14.9m. She was sold in 1977, and
renamed *Cortes*. She was again renamed as *Lady M A Crosbie* in 1978; *Dauphine*, 1984; *Sheryn M*,
1995; *Blue Dolphin*, 1999; *Jull II*, 2002.

The ro-ro ship *Baltic Progress* (1974/4,668grt) maintained a weekly service from Purfleet to Rotterdam and Helsinki with a sister ship *Baltic Eagle*. She measures 137.5m x 22.3m, had a top speed of 17 knots, and carries twelve passengers. She was sold in 1992 and renamed *Tyne Progress*. She was also renamed *Parkhaven* in 1994, Veerhaven in 1998 and *Strofades II,* also in 1998.

September 1994 heralded the official opening of Thames Europort, formerly the Dartford International Ferry Terminal. A twice-daily freight service to Vlissingen by Sally Freight was transferred from Ramsgate, one of the first ships employed being *Sally Sun* (1979/1,528grt), ex-*Gute*, bought by the Sally company in 1992. She could carry sixty driver-accompanied trailers. Soon larger vessels were introduced to the service with the formation of Dart Line, and *Sally Sun* was sold to Swedish owners and renamed *Sea Wind II*.

Maersk Anglia (1977/6,862grt) passes Tilbury, inward bound for Ford's works at Dagenham. She measures 122.94m x 21.04m, has a top speed of 15 knots and carries ninety trailers and 283 TEU. She was renamed *Maersk Kent* in 2000 and *Kent* in 2001. Her previous names were *Admiral Caribe* and *Admiral Nigeria* from 1977 to 1979, *Admiral Caribe* to 1982, *Saint Remy* to 1986 and *Duke of Anglia* to 1990.

Chartered from the Estonian Shipping Company, *Dart 6* joined Dart Line's Thames Europort to Vlissingen service in 1999. She was built in Spain as *Varbola*, weighs 7,606grt, measures 122.32m x 19.80m and has a top speed of 17 knots. She has 1,140 lane metres and twelve berths for vehicle drivers, and carries up to 266 TEU.

Another member of Dart Line's ever-expanding ro-ro fleet is the 9,088grt *Dart 3* which carries up to forty-nine cars, ninety-four trailers and 450 TEU. Completed in 1984, her registered owners are Rosal SA and she flies the flag of the Bahamas. She measures 120m x 21m and has two cargo decks. She was formerly *Balder Stern* to 1985, *Bazias 3* to 1993, *Sally Euroroute* to 1996 and *Merle* to 2000.

Amandine (1978/14,715grt), employed on Cobelfret's ro-ro services from Purfleet and Dagenham to near-Continental ports. She measures 172.95m x 21.73m and has space for 120 cars and 802 TEU. Built at Kiel as *Merzario Persia*, she was renamed *Persia* in 1986, *Buafoss* in 1988 and *Vega* in 1996, acquiring her present name in 1998.

A member of a new class of smart-looking ro-ro ships built in Japan for Cobelfret, the 23,987grt *Valentine* loads at Purfleet for another of her daily voyages to Zeebrugge. Completed in 1999, she measures 162.49m x 25.20m with a top speed of 17.8 knots. She has four vehicle decks, including two in her superstructure, enabling her to carry 635 cars.

Under charter by Cobelfret for their Purfleet–Zeebrugge run, the 10,171grt *Seahawk* has sailed under several names during her career. Launched as *Tor Caledonia* in 1975, she was named *Fichtelberg* until 1991, *Spirit of Dublin* and *Fichtelberg* again in 1992, *Norcliff* until 1993, back to *Fichtelberg* until 1995 and *Dana Minerva* to 1997. She measures 137.55m x 20.60m, with space for 600 cars and 327 TEU. Her top speed is 18.5 knots.

Berthed at Tilbury Container Services in Northfleet Hope in her role as a container feeder ship, the Gibraltar-registered *Euro Melody* (1993/3,992grt) can carry 509 TEU, 366 of which are on deck. She is 99.95m long. She was formerly *Frieda* to 1993, *Scandinavian Bridge* 1993–99, *Frieda* to 2002 and *Melody* to April 2003 when she acquired her current name.

It was in April 1995 that Cobelfret began deploying vessels between Ford Motor Company's Dagenham plant and Zeebrugge. *Eglantine* (1990/10,035grt) lies alongside Ford's jetty awaiting her load of 300 cars and 100 trailers.

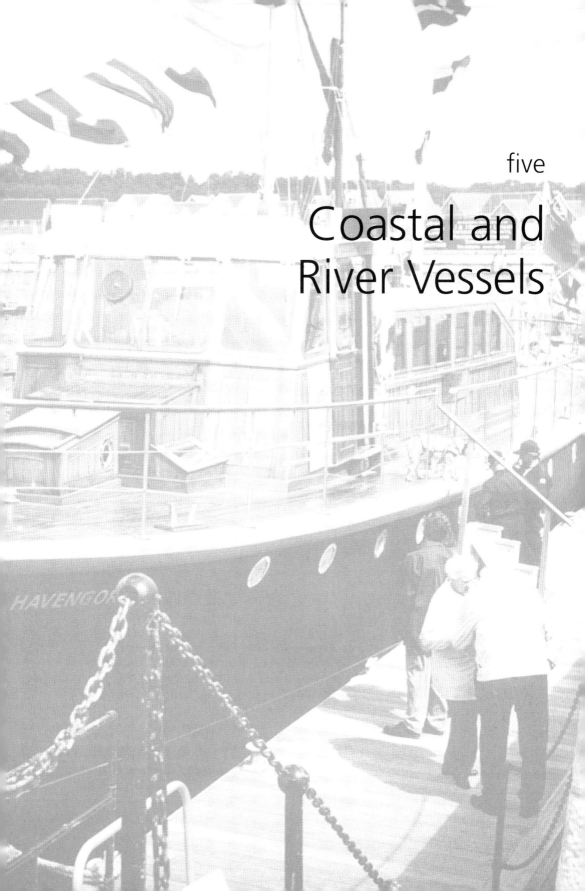

five

Coastal and
River Vessels

'Flatties', 'toshers', 'Bovril boats' – the Port of London's own local characters. But where did they go? The closing of London's docks and power stations, new regulations concerning the disposal of London's sludge and technological advances in ship propulsion all made an impact on these and other vessels which had become everyday sights within the port.

In the middle of the last century, there were around 150 colliers, of which forty were flat-iron colliers, or 'flatties' as they were affectionately known, so-called because their design allowed them to pass under central London's bridges with funnel and mast lowered. Colliers would bring coal from the north-east of England to London's power stations and gasworks, the 'flatties' sailing as far upstream as Wandsworth Gasworks, more than six miles above London Bridge, passing under sixteen low bridges on their way. As power stations and gasworks reduced in numbers and with some stations turning to oil, the colliers were sold off. The very last Central London power station, Lots Road at Chelsea, was decommissioned in 2002, while Tilbury's large downriver coal-fired station is served by bulk carriers nowadays.

The disappearance of the many thousands of lighters from the Port of London scene following the closure of docks and wharves led to the redundancy of river lighterage tugs and 'toshers'. Fortunately a few lighterage tugs have found work pulling barges containing central London's discarded rubbish, but most of them, together with the smaller 'toshers', have fallen by the wayside. Their larger sisters, the towage tugs, were indispensable, pulling, pushing and cajoling every visiting deep-sea ship to and from its berth. The invention of the bow thrust, though, gave new independence to the modern-day ship, and today many vessels sail in and out of the river without tug assistance, subject to weather and tidal conditions. This has contributed to the depletion of the Thames towage-tug fleet, although those which do remain are more powerful and manoeuvrable than ever before.

For more than a hundred years London's sewage waste was disposed of at sea by specially built sludge carriers which became better known as the 'Bovril boats'. Their green hulls would constantly ply the Thames' waters, but a directive from Brussels during the 1990s concerning the dumping of the waste at sea eventually brought to an end their valuable contribution to the health of the capital. The waste is now burned in two large incinerators, creating enough electrical energy to supply an average-sized town.

Small coastal tankers, some of which were built for government use during the Second World War, were employed for many years in the moving of oil products from Thames refineries and installations to storage depots and power stations on the river or direct to ships' bunkers within the port. A fleet of river craft, providing oil and fresh water, still service large ships coming into the Port of London, but the typical modern coastal tanker is much larger and more technically advanced than any of its predecessors, including, like the large ocean tanker, the provision of Flammable Gas Detection equipment.

Memories of old: A steam lighterage tug pulls her cargo-filled lighters past a forest of cranes populating a typical riverside wharf.

Wartime-built coastal tankers regularly plied their trade in Thames waters up until the 1960s. *BP Distributor* (1944/810grt) was owned by Shell Mex & BP Ltd. She measured 61.6m long, and had a top speed of 10 knots. She was built as *Empire Trottwood*, ex-*Amir*, 1947-1952. She was scrapped at Willebrook in 1965.

One of the larger colliers transporting coal from the north-east of England into the Port of London in the days before the demise of the majority of its riverside power stations was *Barford* (1950/3,357grt). She was owned by the Central Electricity Generating Board (CEGB) and had steam-reciprocating engines. She was broken-up by P&W MacLellan Ltd, Bo'ness, in 1972.

An example of London's famous 'flatties' was the 1,771grt *Battersea*, completed in 1951 for the British Electrical Authority, later under the ownership of CEGB. She measured 82.4m x 12m and her top speed was 12.5 knots. She was sold to British owners in 1980 when Battersea Power Station closed, and renamed *Grainville*. She sank in Irish Sea on 14 December 1981 with the loss of three lives.

High and dry: Pre-war-built Sun tugs of W.H.J. Alexander Ltd at St John's Wharf. Powered by steam-reciprocating engines, these older vessels were replaced by the 1960s by more powerful motor tugs.

One of the last middle-sized colliers to be built for CEGB was *James Rowan* (1955/2,947grt). She measured 103.6m x 13.3m, had a top speed of 11 knots, and was broken-up at Queenborough, Kent in 1984.

The disposal at sea of London's sludge dated back to 1887 and the pioneer vessel *Bazalgette*. A later version of the 'Bovril boats', as the Greater London Council's sludge carriers became affectionately known, was the *Sir Joseph Bazalgette*, 2,258grt, built in 1963. Her length was 89m. Constructed with longitudinal framing, she had three holds and saw service until the mid-1980s.

The *Thames* (1977/2,663grt) proved to be the last of the 'Bovril boats' built for the GLC when sludge disposal at sea ceased on 30 December 1998. Seen here during an overhaul, the 93m-long vessel had a service speed of 12 knots and would make two trips per day to her North Sea disposal point.

The little motor tug *Robertsbridge* was typical of the small lighterage tugs which would journey up and down the Thames with their long line of lighters behind them. Owned by Thames & General Lighterage Ltd she weighed just 90grt and dated back to 1937, though she was re-engined in 1962.

St Mawes was originally the Thames towage tug *Ionia*, built in 1960 for William Watkins Ltd who became part of London Tugs in 1969 and the Alexandra Towing Co. in 1975. She measures 30.47m x 7.92m. She was sold to Falmouth Towing Co. in 1987, acquiring her present name in 1988, and returned to the Thames/Medway area in 2003.

The motorised barge *Humber Progress* (1980/380grt) receiving discharged raw sugar cane from the freighter *Avlis* at the Tate & Lyle terminal for onward shipment. Owned by John H. Whitaker, her top speed was 9 knots.

Another of the many small wartime coastal tankers, the 667grt *Asperity* was built as *Empire Dweller* for the Ministry of War Transport in 1942. She measured 56m long and her top speed was 9 knots. She was a member of F.T. Everard Shipping Company's dry-cargo and tanker fleet until May 1967 when she was broken-up in Belgium.

In complete contrast, Everard's latest *Asperity*, completed in 1997 and christened alongside HMS *Belfast*, has been constructed with a double hull and can accomplish three-hour turnarounds as all cargo and ballast control operations are carried out from the bridge. She weighs 2,965grt, measures 88.76m x 16.50m and has five tanks and seven crew.

A typical sand-suction dredger of her day, the 1,317grt *Bowqueen* entered service in 1963. Owned by British Dredging (Shipping) Ltd, she was part of a fleet of similar vessels whose names were prefixed *Bow*. She capsized and sank off Essex coast in September 1965 with the loss of four lives. Raised and reconstructed, she continued to serve the Port of London until 1988 when sold to Portuguese owners, and renamed *Susana Christina*. She is registered at Funchal, Madeira.

The motor tug *Sun XX* (1957/192grt) gave valuable service within the Port of London for twenty-two years. She was built for W.H.J. Alexander Ltd (Sun Tugs) and owned by London Tugs from 1969 and Alexandra Towing Co. from 1975, following company changes. She was sold to Italian owners in May 1979, and renamed *Sole Secondo*.

Almost dwarfed by the heavy-looking load she is pulling, a small tug makes gallant headway past Tilbury. Although the days of the traditional lighter tug are long gone, jobs can usually be found for the few little Thames motor tugs still in service today.

Arco Beck (1989/3,325grt), a modern purpose-built trailing-suction dredger designed to extract sand and gravel from the seabed to depths of up to forty-five metres measures 99.63m x 17.03m. She self-discharges up to 2,000 tons per hour, and her top speed is 12.5 knots. She was formerly *Cambeck* to 1997. She is owned by ARC Marine Ltd who took over the ship's original owners, Civil & Marine Ltd, in 1995.

Pictured in her early days with a skiff, *Havengore* was built by Tough's boatyard at Teddington in 1956 and employed by the Port of London Authority to carry out hydrographical surveys in the Thames Estuary. The 25.9m-long vessel found fame in 1965 when she was chosen to carry Sir Winston Churchill's coffin on the Thames during his state funeral. After being taken out of service, *Havengore's* condition deteriorated and she was put up for sale by the PLA in 1995 to be purchased by the Havengore Trust, specially formed for her restoration.

One of three identical vessels employed on the Woolwich Free Ferry service, *Ernest Bevin* (1963/739grt) can carry up to 200 tons of vehicles together with 1,050 passengers. She measures 56.52m x 21.34m. Like her sisters, she never ties up at the end of each crossing, but is held in position against the piers by her Voith-Schneider propulsion system.

Above: Hoo Finch (1989/794grt) a modern dry-bulk coaster owned by R. Lapthorn & Co., based at Hoo, near Rochester. She carries a wide variety of cargoes such as grain, fertilizers, coal, steel, clay and stone, and measures 58.27m x 9.50m. In 2003 figures showed that there were just forty-eight British-registered coasters under 2,500 tons, of which no less than half were owned by the Lapthorn group.

Opposite below: Now fully restored and based at Chatham, Kent, *Havengore* is always a welcome visitor at maritime events. She is regarded today as a floating memorial to Sir Winston Churchill, travelling around Britain and the Continent and able to accommodate up to ten students studying modern history.

Bruce Stone (1964/357grt) of Thames Shipping Services, moored off Gravesend. She measures 43.7m x 9.2m. She is one of a fleet of small river tankers which are employed in transporting gas oil, waste oil and in ship bunkering.

An example of the latest breed of highly manoeuvrable tractor tugs, *Sun Thames* (1982/330grt) returns downriver to her Gravesend base after making a sojourn into the Pool of London. Behind her is a close sister *Sun Sussex* (1992/378grt). Both vessels were built for the Alexandra Towing Company who were taken over by Australian company Howard Smith Ltd in 1993. In 2001 Howard Smith became part of another Australian company, Adsteam Ltd, whose fleet comprises just five large towage tugs and three smaller tugs, a far cry from 1975 when Alexandra moved in to buy London Tugs' fleet of twenty tugs.

Two self-discharging sand dredgers owned by UMD City of London Ltd transport aggregates from designated banks in the North Sea and English Channel upriver to Murphy's Wharf at Charlton. *City of Westminster* (1990/3,914grt), above, and *City of London* (1989/3,660grt) each have a length of 99.8m and a service speed of 12.5 knots.

The motor tug *Merit* (1964/83grt) is one of seven tugs employed by Cory Environmental to haul lighters of compacted waste downriver from central London. The tugs are descendants of the tug and lighter fleet of William Cory Lighterage which closed down in 1983.

Built as the *Will Everard*, the *Will* is the only survivor of a quartet of steel-hulled spritsail barges completed 1925–26 for F.T. Everard & Sons of Greenhithe. She carried her cargoes along the Thames estuary, sailed to the Medway and coastal towns and competed in Thames barge matches. Her length is 29.86m, her height to masthead 34.14m and she weighs 187grt. She was sold in 1967 and acquired by two private owners before Overseas Containers Ltd (now P&O) took her over as a sales promotion and hospitality vessel.

The fresh water tanker *Aquatic* (1964/199grt) operated by Thames Shipping Services. She measures 35.1m x 7.5m with a top speed of 9 knots. She is another small river vessel which has given invaluable service within the Port of London over the years, as visiting cruise ships are supplied with up to 1,000 tons of fresh water while they are in port.

Hoo Venture (1982/671grt), a *Hoo Willow* class of coastal cargo vessel owned by R. Lapthorn & Co. Ltd, measures 49.99m x 9.40m with a 4.05m draught, single hold, and a top speed of 9 knots. Ships of the Lapthorn fleet have been involved in the carriage of aggregates on the Thames in recent years.

Thames river cruises were revived in 1978 when the world's last seagoing paddle steamer departed from Tilbury Landing Stage for Southend, Margate and Deal. Since then the 693grt *Waverley*, built in 1947 for service on the Clyde, has cruised the Thames virtually every summer as part of her annual round–Britain schedule. In 1974 she was saved from certain extinction by the Paddle Steamer Preservation Society, who, with help from the Heritage Lottery Fund, spent more than £4 million on a major rebuild in 2000 to ensure her long-term future.

Viewed from a ship moored in the Upper Pool, a small river tug hauls her load downstream towards Tower Bridge.

The only full-time excursion ship sailing the Thames between its estuary and central London, Gravesend-based *Princess Pocahontas* was built in Germany as the *Laboe* for employment as a Kiel field riverbus. She was later based at Flensburg and purchased at Cuxhaven in 1989 by her present owner John Potter, a freeman of the Thames. She is used for summer-season day excursions and private charter.

The welcoming party: Thames fireboats spray watercannon in traditional celebration of a new arrival in the Port of London.

six

A Changing Face

The scurrying commuter or lingering tourist who takes in a river view from London Bridge in this present age of the twenty-first century witnesses the culmination of some remarkable changes which have taken place in just a few decades. Smart riverboats, their multi-lingual commentaries rising into the London air, emerge from under the bridge, making their way towards HMS *Belfast*, now an established local resident. Foliage, ornamental lighting and seats adorn quayside walkways, and distinctive brick-built warehouses have been transformed into expensive city business and residential properties. Yet there is still something missing: the ships. Nowadays the bascules of Tower Bridge only go up for the occasional cruise ship or a warship on a courtesy call. No longer can passers-by watch their fruit, butter and bacon being unloaded from cargo vessels seemingly within touching distance of London Bridge. The tall swinging cranes which lowered their jibs in respect as Sir Winston Churchill's funeral procession moved past from Tower Pier have all gone.

Between Woolwich and the Pool of London, balconied apartment blocks have appeared both on the river banks and within the former enclosed docks, either converted from old warehouses or built from new, in similar architectural design to the warehouses they have replaced. Further downstream, occasional wharves and ro-ro terminals are separated by rather colourless stretches of river, void of frequent shipping, until the Port of Tilbury offers the chance to see the largest freighters and cruise ships which enter the Thames. Ship-spotters at Gravesend will certainly not fill their notepads as if they were in the 1960s, but daily periods of activity normally feature impressively large container and ro-ro ships from all over the world.

Leisure and tourism are paramount for the future of the upper areas of the Port of London, especially within the Pool where a multi-million pound regeneration project has been ongoing for a number of years. Tilbury has shown a steady increase in shipping traffic since becoming a free port, while roll-on-roll-off berths at Dartford and Purfleet have, as already described, been a revelation for the port, although, at the time of writing, there are plans to develop vast new facilities downstream on the former site of Shellhaven in an area known as the Thames Gateway. Only the future will tell whether ro-ro and container business is moved even further away from London.

The loss of so many of London's docks, wharves and connected businesses had a huge impact on the lives of river and dock workers, most of whom had to find other employment. In 1959, no less than eighty per cent of cargo tonnage brought into the port was loaded into lighters, ensuring employment for 5,500 lightermen. Today, only around forty lightermen are working within the port. Some workers fortunately found new careers on the Thames, involving themselves with the ever-expanding pleasure-boat industry or helping to preserve former coastal and river craft. There are a number of small vessels receiving constant preservation work with a view to their employment either as static attractions or in running promotional and leisure trips.

This final chapter takes us on an upriver voyage from Gravesend to central London, passing landmarks old and new and observing many of the notable changes made to this stretch of the Thames and to London's retired docks. These changes, like changes everywhere, have not been met without controversy, although according to the PLA twenty-nine wharves upstream from the Thames Barrier have been safeguarded by the Government to prevent redevelopment for anything other than port use. The Port of London still has a rosy future.

The 283grt ferry *Edith* leaving Gravesend's Town Pier which for many years was the landing point on the south side of the Thames for the Gravesend-Tilbury ferry. *Edith* was built in 1911 and after a career spanning fifty years she was broken-up in Belgium in 1961.

Now the oldest surviving cast-iron pier in the world, the Town Pier at Gravesend has been completely refurbished to its former glory. Built in 1834 at a cost of just £8,700, the pier fell into disrepair following its closure to the ferries but was taken over by the local council in 2000. It is pictured before the installation of new bar and restaurant facilities.

Tilbury Landing Stage as it appears today. At 348m long, it was opened on 16 May 1930, becoming the last piece of olde England for many thousands of people emigrating to the antipodes. Passenger-ship calls reached their peak in the 1960s. After extensive modernisation in 1989 and a name change, there was an initial surge in cruise-ship calls, but quiet scenes like this are more common nowadays, especially away from the summer months.

Even Cunard showed an interest in using the upgraded cruise facilities at Tilbury, bringing their 24,492grt vessel *Vistafjord* into the Thames. These plans did not develop though, the ship being renamed *Caronia* and cruising out of Southampton before being sold to Saga.

Access for shipping into the Port of Tilbury is via an entrance lock through which the first ship passed on 26 September 1929. Measuring 304.80m long and 33.53m wide, it allowed in its early days the largest vessels afloat to enter the docks. Here, the cruise ship *Fedor Shalyapin*, led by a Howard Smith tug, continues her inward journey to her berth at Tilbury.

The extended riverside berths of Tilbury's Northfleet Hope Container Terminal. Independently operated by Tilbury Container Services Ltd (TCS) under the joint ownership of P&O Ports, Associated British Ports and Forth Ports plc, its riverside berths have a minimum draught of 12.5m and are equipped with three single-lift and two twin-lift Paceco container-handling cranes. Berths 39 and 41 inside Port of Tilbury's docks are also under the control of TCS.

Immediately upstream from the container facilities in Northfleet Hope, Tilbury Grain Terminal opened in 1969 as an import facility. Further premises (seen to the right) were later built downstream where they could receive grain direct from ships and silos. On this occasion the modern short-sea Irish cargo ship *Arklow River* is moored alongside. The main jetty length is 274.3m, the coaster jetty 70m.

Now a major landmark within the bounds of the Port of London, the Queen Elizabeth II Bridge cost £86 million to construct and was opened on 30 October 1991. The 2,872m structure carries motorway traffic between the counties of Essex and Kent and its navigational clearance of 57.5m enables the largest ships wishing to moor further upstream to pass easily underneath.

At Lavender Wharf, one of the many oil-storage depots which used to populate the Thames riverside, Everard's coastal tanker *Austility* (1946/933grt) prepares to return downriver having discharged her cargo of oil products.

Free and easy: since the first crossing of a Woolwich ferry on 23 March 1889 no charge has ever been imposed for the convenience of using this well-known link between the north and south banks of the Thames. Throughout the time only three generations of ferries have carried passengers, vehicles, goods and animals across this stretch of water, and the present trio, of which two are shown here, have been plying their trade for more than forty years, witnessing many changes to river life along the way.

The Dagenham works of the Ford Motor Company with a ro-ro ship berthed at its jetty. Ships now sail twice a day to Zeebrugge from the jetty which holds over 1,000 cars for shipment.

Spillers Flour Mills were located in Royal Victoria Dock, part of the Royal Docks system, and would be served by ocean vessels such as the 1950s freighter *Continental Merchant*. Today the western end of Royal Victoria Dock has been turned into a water-sports centre, while jet aircraft constantly take-off and land at London City Airport, constructed on the old quaysides between Royal Albert and King George V Docks.

Opposite: The decorative bow and figurehead of *Cutty Sark*, testimony to the skills of the craftsmen who built her. The world's sole-surviving tea clipper, she was launched at Dumbarton in 1869 and now sits proudly in her personal dry-dock at Greenwich. Open daily to the public.

In front of the expansive riverside warehouses of Orient Wharf, *Weno*, a pre-war steam tug, has arrived with more lighters.

Two old stalwarts of the Port of London: *Swiftstone* (1952/91grt) worked as a lighterage tug for Cory's until replaced by a new vessel in 1998. She is now managed by a charitable trust and remains in good working order. *Massey Shaw*, a former Thames fireboat, gave sterling service during the Second World War, being involved in the London Blitz and making three round trips from England to the Dunkirk beaches, bringing back 106 men. Retiring from Thames service in 1971, she was initially badly neglected, but thankfully has since been lovingly restored.

The modern face of the Port of London: the controversial Millennium Dome, still, at the time of writing, awaiting further use, with the buildings of Canary Wharf behind.

The 94grt *Portwey*, a twin-screwed coal-fired tug built in 1927 and seeing service at Falmouth and Weymouth. She is in her original condition, although restoration work is continuing. She is owned by ST Portwey Trust and based at West India Quay in London Docklands.

Above: In the week of its 100th
birthday Tower Bridge opens for the
excursion ship *Balmoral*. Between the
bascules can be seen RY *Britannia* and
the cruise ship *Seabourn Pride*, guests at
the celebrations.

Right: General Marine's small motor
tug *Revenge* (1948/61grt) re-enacts an
old rule of the river by assisting a
pleasure steamer through Tower Bridge
and into the Upper Pool. A condition
of Tower Bridge's construction in the
late-nineteenth century stated that a tug
should be kept on permanent standby
should a vessel require assistance. The
provision of the Tower Bridge Tug, as
it became known, remained until the
late 1960s when much of the Pool's
commercial trade ceased.

HMS *Belfast*, the first warship since HMS *Victory* to be preserved for the nation, arrived in the Upper Pool on 14 October 1971. She is now a principal tourist attraction and acts as a mooring for visiting cruise ships and other vessels. Launched in 1938, her displacement is 13,175 tons and she measures 187m x 19.7m. She was repainted in her North Atlantic camouflage colours in 1993.

Behind the original brick façade of Hay's Wharf the dock where tea clippers once moored has been sealed to form Hay's Galleria, opened in 1988 and featuring shops, restaurants and stalls. The wharf became a centre for importing dairy produce before the advent of container ships in the 1960s when it fell into disrepair. Nowadays it forms part of London Bridge City, an imaginative development comprising residential and commercial property.

This attractive wall plaque at Hay's Galleria informs visitors of the former wharf's fascinating history.

Above: A scene that epitomises the upper regions of the Port of London in the twenty-first century: the river cruiser *Mercia* was purchased from Germany to meet increasing demands for Thames pleasure trips. Behind her, Butlers Wharf, once a cluster of bustling warehouses, offers residential and office space and swish eating places.

Below: St Katharine Docks closed for business in 1968, the warehouses in the docks' Eastern Basin never having been replaced since their devastation during the London Blitz in September 1940. Restoration of the docks began as early as the 1970s and they are now on the map as St Katharine's Yacht Haven, a thriving retail, commercial and residential development with a marina and, as seen here, a base for several Thames sailing barges which can be chartered for corporate hospitality.

Another view of St Katharine Docks, featuring its busy marina, home to private craft of all shapes and sizes.

One of several retired vessels which have found new careers at their central London moorings, the 556grt paddle steamer *Tattershall Castle* was built in 1934 and worked for the British Railways Board as a Humber ferry until 1973. In 1975 she moved to the Victoria Embankment, opening as an art gallery and conference centre, but is now a floating restaurant and bar. She measures 63.70m x 17.37m.

A look back to 30 January 1965 – *Havengore's* big day. The PLA launch makes her solemn journey from Tower Pier to Festival Pier with the coffin of Sir Winston Churchill. In the background, her decks lined with servicemen, is HMS *Chrysanthemum*, owned by an educational charity and moored at the Victoria Embankment until 1988. Built as a Royal Navy sloop in 1918, she also found fame, appearing in the film *Indiana Jones and the Last Crusade*.

Much of modern London's life revolves around its river. Here, a luxurious new river-excursion boat glides past the London Eye. Tourism is vital for the future of this length of the Thames now that the power stations and most riverside wharves have closed.

No apologies for returning to the finest sight in the Port of London; the opening of Tower Bridge creates much excitement even to this day.

Before ending this book mention must be made of the Museum in Docklands, opened on 24 May 2003 after many years of hard graft by its instigators. Located on five floors in No.1 Warehouse West India Quay in London's Docklands, it covers the history of London's river, port and people from Roman times to the building of the Docklands development in the latter years of the last century.

Other local titles published by Tempus

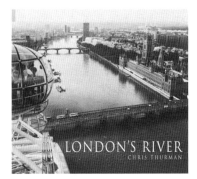

London's River Westminster to Woolwich
CHRIS THURMAN

The River Thames has been the lifeblood of London since before Roman times. It is its *raison d'être* and has been responsible for the growth of this remarkable city. This book captures the many changes along the river over the last forty years.
0 7524 2595 1

London Life in the Post-War Years
DOUGLAS WHITWORTH

A collection of evocative photographs taken in London in the immediate post-war years, showing some of the best-known sights in the capital, including Blitz damage, Oxford Street shop windows, the Festival of Britain and the Coronation decorations.
0 7524 2816 0

The Port of Medieval London
GUSTAV MILNE

It was during the later medieval period that London grew to become the largest town in the land. Participating in extensive excavations of the London waterfront enabled Gustav Milne to describe the changing appearance of the town and its ships and merchants over the long period from 600 to 1500. The resulting picture is a vivid reconstruction of the working port of London, the dynamic engine of the medieval economy.
0 7524 2544 7

Waverley Paddler for a Pound
DOUGLAS McGOWAN

Waverley, the world's last seagoing paddle steamer, was destined for the scrapyard in 1974 when Douglas McGowan and the Paddle Steamer Preservation Society purchased her for the princely sum of £1 and the rest is, as they say, history. Fresh from a £7M refit in Great Yarmouth, *Waverley* is resplendent in her black, red and white livery and can be seen sailing the coast of Britain again.
0 7524 2877 2

If you are interested in purchasing other books published by Tempus, or in case you have difficulty finding any Tempus books in your local bookshop, you can also place orders directly through our website

www.tempus-publishing.com

or from **BOOKPOST**, Freepost, PO Box 29, Douglas, Isle of Man, IM99 1BQ
tel 01624 836000   email bookshop@enterprise.net